THE ANGLO-SAXONS

Roger Coote

Thomson Learning
New York

Look into the Past

The Anglo-Saxons
The Aztecs
The Greeks
The Egyptians
The Romans
The Vikings

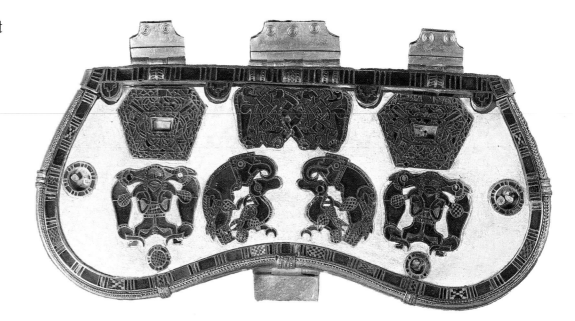

First published in the
United States in 1994 by
Thomson Learning
115 Fifth Avenue
New York, NY 10003

First published in 1993
by Wayland (Publishers) Ltd.

Library of Congress Cataloging-in-Publication Data
Coote, Roger.
  The Anglo-Saxons / Roger Coote.
       p.   cm. — (Look into the past)
  Originally published: Wayland, 1993.
  Includes bibliographical references and index.
  ISBN 1-56847-062-2 : $14.95
  1. Great Britain — History — Anglo-Saxon period, 449–
1066 — Juvenile literature. 2. Anglo-Saxons — Juvenile
literature. [1. Great Britain — History — Anglo-Saxon
period, 449–1066. 2. Anglo-Saxons.] I. Title. II. Series.
DA152.2.C66   1994
942.01 — dc20   93-34486

Printed in Italy

Picture acknowledgments
The publishers wish to thank the following for providing the
photographs for this book: Lesley & Roy Adkins Picture
Library 9 (top), 15; Ancient Art and Architecture Collection
7 (both), 13, 20 (top), 23 (top), 27 (top); Bodleian Library,
Oxford 14 (bottom); British Library 11 (both), 12 (both),
16, 29 (bottom); reproduced by courtesy of the Trustees of
the British Museum 17 (bottom); C. M. Dixon 21 (top), 23
(bottom), 24 (bottom), 25 (bottom), 26; E. T. Archive
5 (top), 10, 14 (top); Robert Harding Picture Library
5 (bottom), 8, 18, 19, 22; Michael Holford 24 (top), 25 (top),
27 (bottom); Hulton Deutsch Collection 17 (top);
Syndication International 28, 29 (top).
Artwork by Peter Bull 4; Jenny Hughes 6; Stephen Wheele 9.

Contents

Words that appear in **_bold italic_** in the text are explained in the glossary on page 30.

WHO WERE THE ANGLO-SAXONS?

The Anglo-Saxons were people who came from many different tribes in northern Germany and Denmark to settle in Britain. The first Anglo-Saxons came as traders or as soldiers in the Roman army. When the Romans left Britain in A.D. 410, more and more Anglo-Saxons came to settle in the country. At first they lived in areas that were not inhabited by the people who already lived in Britain – called the Britons. Later, they began to conquer the Britons, calling their land England, land of the Angles.

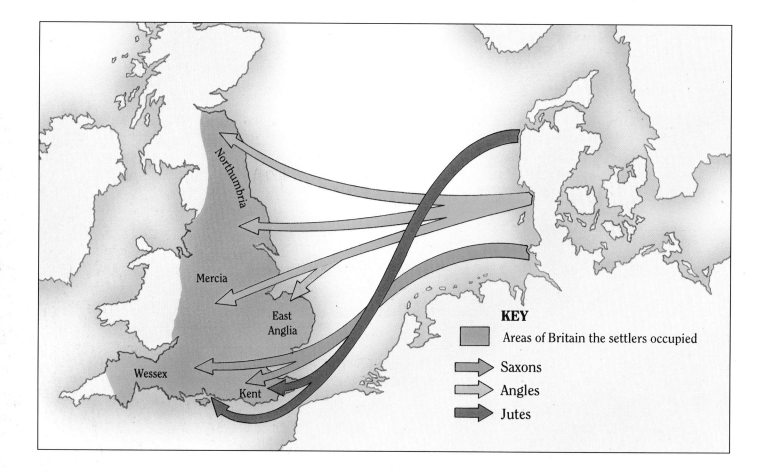

KEY

Areas of Britain the settlers occupied

Saxons

Angles

Jutes

This map shows the routes taken by the Anglo-Saxons who invaded and settled in Britain. They came from tribes of Jutes, Angles, and Saxons, and they are usually known simply as Anglo-Saxons. They settled first along the east and south coasts and then moved inland. As they spread out, they either conquered the native Britons or pushed them farther and farther west, into Cornwall, Wales, and northwest England.

When the Anglo-Saxons spread inland, they forced the Britons to move west. Sometimes the Anglo-Saxons and the Britons agreed on borders between their lands. But sometimes the Anglo-Saxons simply decided where they wanted the border to be and then built tall earth banks and ditches to mark it. This is Offa's Dike, which was built along the border between Mercia (an Anglo-Saxon kingdom) and Wales (which was occupied by the Britons). In some places the earth bank is over 12 feet high. Offa was a powerful king of Mercia, and he ordered the dike to be built in the late eighth century. ▼

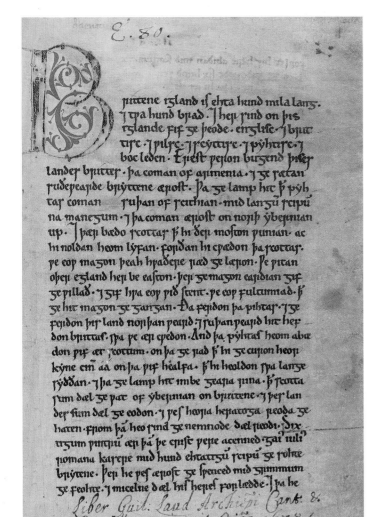

▲ There is a book called the *Anglo-Saxon Chronicle*, which tells us a lot about how and when the Anglo-Saxons arrived in Britain. It was written after their invasion as a record of events and was updated regularly, like a diary. This is a page from the beautiful, handwritten *Chronicle*.

CHIEFTAIN, CHURL, AND SLAVE

Most Anglo-Saxons lived in small settlements. Each settlement had its own lord, and a group of settlements was ruled by a local chieftain or king. At first, England had a great many small kingdoms. As time went on, some kingdoms became more powerful and took over the lands of neighboring kings. Eventually, there were just seven kingdoms, each with its own king.

These are the seven kingdoms that made up Saxon England. The kingdoms often fought each other and their borders did not stay the same for long. Sometimes the king of the strongest kingdom was recognized by the other kings as their overlord. In the sixth century Kent was the richest and most powerful kingdom. Northumbria became the strongest in the seventh century, and Mercia took over in the eighth century.

NORTHUMBRIA

Offa's Dike

MERCIA

EAST ANGLIA

ESSEX

River Thames

KENT

WESSEX

SUSSEX

During the ninth century, Wessex became the most powerful Anglo-Saxon kingdom. The statue in this picture is of King Alfred, who came to the throne of Wessex in 871 and ruled for twenty-eight years. This was a difficult time for the Anglo-Saxons, because their kingdoms were being attacked by people from Scandinavia – the Danes, or Vikings. ▶

The Danes conquered Northumbria, East Anglia, and parts of Mercia and then threatened to overrun Wessex. But Alfred beat the Danes in battle and won back lands they had conquered. In 878 Alfred made peace with the Danes and agreed to share England with them.

▲ Apart from the king, the people of Anglo-Saxon England were divided into two main groups. There were freemen, who were allowed to own land and could travel around where they wished, and slaves, who belonged to the freemen and had almost no freedom at all. The wealthiest freemen were the king's noblemen, who were called earls or thanes. Most Anglo-Saxons were less wealthy freemen known as churls. Slaves belonged to their master and could not leave unless the master sold them or decided to give them their freedom. In this picture, a slave is holding a horse steady so that his master's wife can climb into the saddle.

AN ANGLO-SAXON VILLAGE

The Anglo-Saxon settlers did not move into the towns and villas left by the Romans. Instead, they built their own villages. Each village consisted of one or more groups of small huts. Each group of huts belonged to a family, which included parents, grandparents, children, aunts, uncles, and slaves. Some huts were for sleeping in and others were workshops or storehouses. At the center of each group of huts was a large hall, where the whole family met to eat and talk.

Anglo-Saxons did not build their houses from stone or brick. They used wooden timbers to construct the strong frame of a hut. Then wooden planks were nailed to the frame to make the walls. Another way of making walls was to weave thin sticks, or wattles, into panels and daub them with a layer of mud mixed with straw to keep out drafts and rain. The roofs of the huts were thatched with straw or reeds. This hut and the hut at the top of page 9 have been built to look like real Anglo-Saxon huts. They are in a village called West Stow, in Suffolk. ***Archaeologists*** have found the remains of an Anglo-Saxon village there.

▼ This illustration shows how a small Anglo-Saxon village might have looked. In the center is the hall, and it is surrounded by dwelling huts and workshops. The village is close to a river so that the people have a good supply of fresh water. The land on which the village was built was once forest, but the villagers cut down the trees and used the wood to build their huts. Wood was also needed to make fences and to use as fuel for heating and cooking. More forest was cut down or burned to make farmland around the village. The land was divided among the villagers and used for growing food.

FARMING

Most Anglo-Saxons worked on the land, growing crops and raising *livestock*. The land around a village was divided into long, thin strips, which were about 1,500 to 2,400 square yards in size. The strips were divided among the villagers, with each farmer having some strips of good, *fertile* land and some poorer land. The strips were then farmed by the "rotation" system, in which a different crop was grown on each strip every year. For example, in the first year oats might be grown on one strip. Barley might take its place in the second year. In the third year the strip would be left fallow – *plowed* but not planted – giving the soil a chance to regain its fertility for the next year's crop.

The lives of the Anglo-Saxons were ruled by the calendar. Most people worked on the land and had to do certain jobs at certain times of the year. In the autumn and winter, land was plowed to prepare for sowing new crops. This plow is being pulled by four oxen. Oxen were very expensive, and they were probably shared by the villagers. Anglo-Saxon plows were heavy and difficult to turn around at the end of a row. The fields were long and narrow so that the plow would not have to be turned too often. The boy on the left is prodding the oxen with a sharp stick to keep them moving. The man behind the plowman is sowing seeds – probably for a cereal crop, such as oats, barley, wheat, or rye.

▲ Other crops besides cereals were grown, including vegetables such as peas, beans, and lentils, flax for making linen, and woad and madder (plants to make dyes for coloring cloth). Most of these were planted during the spring. After the soil had been plowed, there might still be some large lumps of earth to be broken up. In the picture above, the two men on the left are using a spade and a pick to break up the soil, while the man on the right is scattering seeds.

▼ Cereal crops were harvested during the late summer and early autumn. The stalks were cut with curved blades called sickles and the crop was loaded onto carts. Farm animals were allowed into the fields to eat the stubble that was left in the ground after harvesting. The next job was threshing – separating the cereal grains from the husks and stalks. The men in the center of this picture are using tools called **flails** to **thresh** a crop. When the grains had been separated, they could be ground up to make flour.

▲ Anglo-Saxon villagers raised farm animals to provide food and clothing. Cattle and sheep were raised for their meat, milk, and bones. The skin of cattle was used to make leather, and sheep's wool was spun and woven into cloth. Poultry was raised for eggs and meat. Most animals were kept inside during the winter, but at other times of the year they stayed outside. Pigs were usually allowed to roam in the forests and find their own food. The pigs in the picture above are eating acorns that have fallen from oak trees.

▼ Livestock were butchered during the autumn to provide meat during the winter months. The meat was put in barrels and covered with salt to prevent it from going bad. As we can see in the picture below, animals were butchered in a very basic way – one man is holding a goat by the horns to keep it still while the other chops off its head with an ax.

OTHER WORK

Not everyone in an Anglo-Saxon village worked on the land all year round. At the busiest times of the farming year, especially when crops had to be harvested, almost everyone lent a hand. But at other times some people did different jobs. For example, hunters, fowlers, and fishermen caught wild animals, birds, and fish for food; blacksmiths made weapons and tools from iron; and potters made clay pots for cooking and storing food.

The man in the picture is a fowler. He is using a hawk to catch birds. A fowler captured young hawks each spring and trained them to catch smaller birds with their claws and bring them back to him. Then, in autumn, the fowler set his hawks free so that he would not have to feed them through the winter. The fowler also had other ways of catching birds. He used **snares**, traps, nets, or a sticky mixture called birdlime, made from plants. The fowler smeared birdlime on tree branches and twigs so that small birds would stick to it when they landed.

Every Anglo-Saxon
settlement probably
had at least one
blacksmith. Smiths
were responsible for
making a huge variety
of iron items. These
included swords,
knives, spearheads, ax
heads, sickles, belt
buckles, brooches,
locks and keys, bowls,
buckets, cups, and
spoons. Clearly, the
blacksmith had to be
very skilled to be able
to make so many
different things, and
he must have been a
very important person
14 in the village.

This picture shows a replica of an Anglo-Saxon weaving *loom*. Both wool and flax were woven into cloth, although wool was more important. As well as making cloth for themselves, Anglo-Saxons also exported cloth to other countries. It may be that all girls were taught how to weave when they were young and that most clothes were made in the home. Archaeologists have found that some settlements were weaving-villages, perhaps making cloth for trade. In these villages, there were a number of buildings that were used as weaving sheds and others in which the wool and finished cloth were stored.

FOOD

y modern standards, Anglo-Saxon meals were probably not very exciting to eat. People ate what they could grow in their own fields or catch for themselves. Most everyday food was boiled or stewed in *cauldrons* hung over a fire. The usual dish was pottage – a cross between a soup and a vegetable stew – which was served with thick slabs of bread. Meat was a luxury and was often eaten only at feasts.

On special days throughout the year, feasts were held in the halls in Anglo-Saxon settlements. In farming villages there would be a feast to celebrate the harvest. Much grander feasts were held in a king's hall, and the nobles would swear their loyalty to their lord and would promise to risk death for him. This picture shows a feast being held in the hall of a wealthy noble. The guests are being served by slaves. They are using knives to eat their food; each guest took his or her own knife to a feast. There was usually a lot of drinking at feasts, with ale and *mead* (made from honey) as the most popular drinks.

These two boys are ▶ cooking chickens and a piglet at a feast. The boy on the right was called a "turnspit," and his job was to turn the long iron bar so that the meat cooked evenly on all sides. The boy on the left is putting logs on to the fire. The Anglo-Saxons ate lots of different types of meat, including beef, *mutton*, pork, and chicken, which they raised on their land; and hare, wild boar, and *venison* from *game* animals caught by hunters. Most game was eaten by wealthy people, because they were the only ones who could afford to have their own hunters or had enough spare time to go hunting themselves.

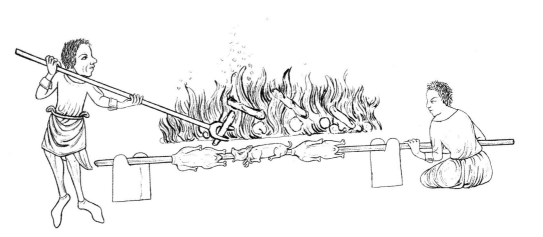

▼ Pottery mugs were normally used for drinking, but at their feasts, many Anglo-Saxons used hollowed-out animal horns. The main drawback was that if the horn was put down the liquid inside spilled out. Gradually, craftsmen became skilled at making glassware and were able to make beautiful drinking glasses, jugs, and bowls. These items were very expensive and were owned by only the wealthiest people.

CLOTHES AND JEWELRY

Anglo-Saxon clothes were made of natural materials that could be obtained by farming and hunting. Wool from sheep and linen from the flax plant were the most commonly used fabrics. Nearly all people wore much the same type of clothes, which were well suited to farm work. Even rich people wore quite simple clothes, although the fabrics may have been of better quality. Children were thought of as small adults so they dressed like their parents.

◀ This picture shows people at a *reconstructed* Anglo-Saxon village at West Stow, in Suffolk. The men are wearing tunics that come down to just above the knee. Underneath, they have thin trousers, or leggings. Some people wore shoes made of leather (from animal skins), although others simply wrapped their feet in pieces of woolen material, which they tied around their ankles. When the weather was very cold, men and boys wore long cloaks and caps.

▲ These people are pretending to be at a feast in an Anglo-Saxon hall. The women in the foreground are wearing tunics similar to those of the men, although they are much longer. The garment with a hood was called a mantle and was worn over a tunic. In cold weather, a second tunic was put on over the mantle. Most women wore their hair long.

The main difference between the clothes of rich people and those of the poor was the jewelry and ornaments that they wore. Most people wore some form of jewelry, but the rich could afford more expensive items. Brooches and clasps were often worn to hold garments together – zippers and snaps had not been invented. Buckles were also worn on straps and belts. These two pictures show Anglo-Saxon jewelry of differing quality.

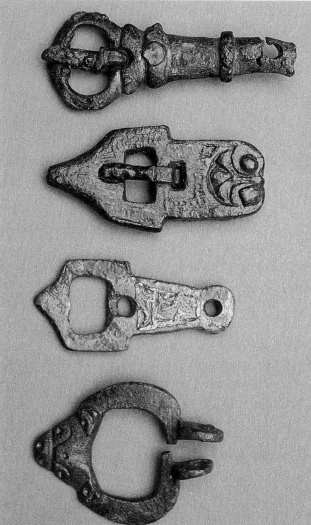

▲ The large, highly decorated gold buckle was found in the grave of a Saxon king, possibly Redwald, who died in 624. He was buried at a place called Sutton Hoo in Suffolk.

◀ The other buckles were found by archaeologists digging at a Saxon settlement. They are made of cheaper metals and are not as skillfully decorated.

At Sutton Hoo, ▶ archaeologists uncovered hundreds of items, including swords, spears, bowls, and nails. Rich jewels were also discovered, many decorated with gold and precious stones. This is one of the king's clasps, which fastened his cloak at his shoulder.

Although the teeth of this comb have been broken off, you can see that the Anglo-Saxons used combs very similar to the ones that we use today.

21

FIGHTING AND WARFARE

Life in Anglo-Saxon England was often violent. In the early part of the Anglo-Saxon period, settlements were sometimes attacked by neighboring chieftains, villagers were killed, and livestock was stolen. The forests that lay between settlements were often home to outlaws who set upon travelers and robbed them. Beginning in the late eighth century, settlements were also attacked by fierce Viking raiders from across the North Sea. Then, in 1066, the Normans invaded from northern France, defeated the Anglo-Saxons, and conquered England.

◀ When a village had to be defended against attack, the villagers would grab their weapons and fight. The most usual weapons were spears, swords, and battle-axes. For protection, some men wore either a leather or *chain mail jerkin* and a helmet, and many carried a round wooden shield. The chain mail was simply put on over the tunic. This man is dressed in much the same way as an Anglo-Saxon fighter might have been.

▲ This scene was carved on the side of a beautifully decorated box, which is known as the Franks casket. It was made in the early eighth century and shows a group of Saxon warriors going into battle. Some of the fighters have spears while others have swords. The spear was most often used by the ordinary men, who might have been called from the fields to defend their village. The sword was the weapon of a noble or other important person.

◄ This is the hilt, or handle, and part of the blade of a Saxon sword found in Yorkshire. It was made in the ninth or tenth century. Most of the sword is of iron, with patterned silver strips on the hilt. The Saxons treasured fine swords and sometimes gave them names. Such weapons were passed down from father to son.

The helmet and the metal decorations on the shield in these pictures were found in the grave at Sutton Hoo. The helmet is made of iron, decorated with other, more valuable, metals including silver. It is extremely large and was probably padded on the inside.

◄ The shield was made of wood and was almost 3 feet across. The wood rotted away over the centuries (the one in the picture is a modern reconstruction), leaving only the metal fittings showing a dragon, a bird of prey, and other objects.

TRADE AND TRAVEL

In Anglo-Saxon times, people traveled only if they had to. Most people stayed in and around their own settlements all their lives. This was partly because most of the things they needed were made or grown nearby. Also, traveling was dangerous. Many roads passed through forests where bandits lived – people such as criminals on the run and men who had lost the protection of their masters and had no way of making a living. Any traveler was a target for attack by these bandits.

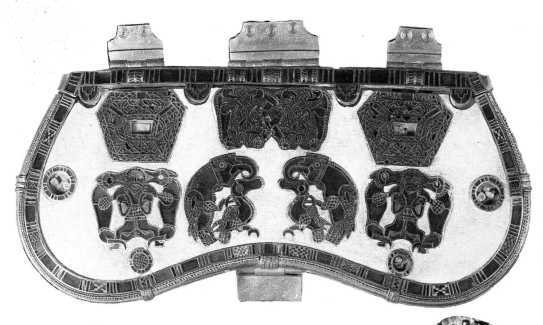

◄ This purse lid was part of the treasure found at Sutton Hoo. The goods found at Sutton Hoo show that there was a great deal of trade between Anglo-Saxon England and mainland Europe: the purse lid was found with gold coins that came from France; the shield and helmet opposite were made in the Swedish style; and there were silver items from the *Byzantine Empire*.

Merchants and *peddlers* traveled around selling goods in towns and villages. People would either buy things, with coins like these, or exchange goods for other goods. ►

RELIGION

The earliest Saxon settlers in England were *pagans* who worshiped a number of gods. The most important gods were Woden, the god of wisdom; Tiw, the god of war; Thunor, the thunder god; and Frig, the goddess of fertility. The Anglo-Saxons offered *sacrifices* to please their gods and tried to use magic spells to get the gods to help them. When the spells were written down, letters called runes were used. In the late sixth century Christian missionaries – including Columba, from Ireland, and Augustine, from Rome – arrived in England. Gradually, they persuaded the Anglo-Saxons to abandon their pagan gods and become Christians.

The bodies of pagan Saxons were often burned and the ashes were then put in special pottery containers called urns. The urn in the picture dates from the sixth century and was found in Lincolnshire. The bodies or ashes of kings and other important Saxons were often placed in ships that were then buried under large mounds of earth. It is thought that Redwald, king of East Anglia, was buried in the famous ship burial at Sutton Hoo. By the time his burial mound was **excavated** in 1939, the wooden ship had rotted away, but its shape could still be seen from marks in the soil.

Christian monks established **monasteries** ▶ where they could live and practice their faith. The monasteries – especially those in the north of England – became important centers of learning, and they were places where reading and writing were taught. The monks made beautiful copies of religious books. The picture shows pages from the Lindisfarne Gospels, which were made near the end of the seventh century. They were written in Latin, and the pages of the book were made from flattened animal skins.

◀ As Christianity spread, the Anglo-Saxons converted their pagan temples into churches. Later, they began building new churches out of stone. This one at Bradford-on-Avon, Wiltshire, was built during the early eighth century and was added to in the tenth century.

LEISURE AND WRITING

For most ordinary Anglo-Saxons, life was very hard and rather short – we learn from burial sites that only a small number lived to be more than forty years old. There was very little time for leisure. The main events to look forward to were probably the feasts in the hall of the village. On these occasions, there would be better food than usual and plenty to drink. Entertainment might be provided by traveling *minstrels*, acrobats, or story-tellers.

The people in this picture are entertainers who traveled from place to place to perform at feasts and for wealthy nobles and kings. They are shown playing many different musical instruments, such as pipes, drums, and a harp. Entertainers such as acrobats, jugglers, and singers were often not much older than children. They might have had to leave home because their parents were too poor to take care of them. Or perhaps they decided that being an entertainer was more interesting than a hard life working on the land.

This is a page from ▶ *Beowulf*, the oldest English poem. It was written between A.D. 700 and 750 (but this copy was made around 1000). The long poem is set in Denmark, and it tells the story of the hero Beowulf, who fights monsters and dragons and becomes king.

▲ The men in this picture are using dogs to hunt a wolf. Other animals hunted by wealthy Anglo-Saxons included stags, wild boars, foxes, and, perhaps, badgers. Fowling with hawks was also a favorite pastime among the rich. Such people often rode horses when they were hunting; it is thought that Saxons also used horses for racing.

GLOSSARY

Archaeologists People who dig up and study objects from the past in order to learn about the civilizations that created them.

Byzantine Empire The eastern part of the Roman Empire, whose capital was Constantinople (now Istanbul in Turkey).

Cauldron A large pot used for cooking food.

Chain mail A type of flexible armor made of metal rings fixed together with rivets.

Excavate To dig up buried ruins.

Fertile Having soil that is rich enough to produce good crops.

Flails Jointed sticks used to beat grain in order to separate it from its husk.

Game Animals and birds that are hunted for sport.

Jerkin A short jacket with no sleeves or collar.

Livestock Farm animals.

Loom A machine for weaving thread into cloth.

Mead Wine made by fermenting honey.

Merchant A person who makes his or her living by buying and selling goods.

Minstrels Traveling musicians.

Monasteries Buildings where monks live.

Mutton Meat from a fully grown sheep.

Pagan A person who is not a Christian, Jew, or Muslim.

Peddler A person who travels from place to place selling goods (usually small items).

Plow To turn over the soil of a field using a metal tool, called a plow, which is dragged through the earth.

Reconstruct In archaeology, to remake a building or other object from the past by piecing together evidence of the way it looked originally.

Sacrifice To offer up something precious, such as an animal, to a god in order to please that god.

Snares Traps to catch animals.

Thresh To separate grain from straw by beating it.

Venison The meat from deer.

IMPORTANT DATES

All these dates are A.D.

410-520? Saxons start to settle in England.

563? The Christian missionary Columba visits Iona, an island off the west coast of Scotland.

597 The Christian missionary Augustine visits England.

681 By now the whole of England is converted to Christianity. The Lindisfarne Gospel is produced.

700? The Franks Casket is made.

700-750? *Beowulf* is written, although the surviving manuscript is dated 1000.

715 Bradford-on-Avon church is built.

730? The monk Bede writes the *Ecclesiastical History of the English People.*

757-796 Offa is King of Mercia.

792 The Vikings raid Lindisfarne.

867 Danes conquer Northumbria and York.

871-899 Alfred is King of Wessex.

871 Danes invade East Anglia and Wessex.

954 England becomes one kingdom under the Danes.

1066 William the Conqueror leads the Norman invasion of England.

BOOKS TO READ

Ellenby, J. *Anglo-Saxon Household.* New York: Cambridge University Press, 1986.

Haynes, Sarah. *Robin Hood.* New York: Henry Holt & Co., 1989.

Reeve, John et al. *Anglo-Saxons.* Jersey City, NJ: Parkwest Publications, 1984.

The Saxons and the Normans. Auburn, ME: Ladybird Books, 1990.

Sutcliff, Rosemary. *Beowulf.* Magnolia, MA: Peter Smith Publishing, 1984.

INDEX